No Milk Today

NO MILK TODAY

Hearty Home-Cooking

without Milk, Citrus or Caffeine

Debbie Cooper

Photographs by Jon Leech

Ashgrove Publishing

London

Contents

Contents

Thank you, Jon, for being my recipe taster and photographer

Introduction

The purpose of this book is to provide quick, easy to make and delicious recipes for families without the use of milk or lactose products. Additionally, cooks can avoid the inclusion of citrus and caffeine ingredients should they wish. This book explains all you need to know about where to go for help and advice and how to select ingredients.

There are recipes and suggestions for soups, starters, light meals, main dishes, fish dishes, vegetarian dishes, savoury sauces, salads, puddings, sweets and treats, baking, pastry, breakfast and beverages.

Some people choose a restricted diet in order to feel more healthy. Others, like myself, who suffer from food intolerances, follow such a diet because it's necessary to maintain health. If you suffer from eczema, asthma, headaches, sinus problems, stomach cramps or bloating, it may well be that reactions to the food that you eat can cause or aggravate these ailments. It can be quite a shock to alter your diet completely, but it does not mean you have to give up enjoying your food. Changing my diet has proved well worthwhile.

If you have family members, or friends, who suffer from an intolerance to milk products, it can be difficult to cook something different just for them. These recipes are meant to be enjoyed by everyone, including the ever growing number of children with food intolerances. Many people will not even realise they are eating, for example, ice-cream without milk! Most of the recipes here are quick and easy to make for everyday meals, whilst others offer ideas for those special occasions.

Supermarkets and health food shops are beginning to stock more specialist ingredients suitable for people with food intolerances. By using these and other readily available products, many meals which in the past had to be avoided can now be made easily at home.

How to Use this Book

Each recipe is milk, citrus and caffeine free. If you do not have to avoid all of these, the recipes offer ways in which they can be adapted to suit your diet. For example, carob can be replaced with milk-free dark chocolate if you do not have a caffeine intolerance.

Reading Labels

It can be difficult to find out what is in our food, so it is very important that you read labels carefully. To save time searching for suitable ingredients, I have found that the products listed below are appropriate for those with a milk, citrus or caffeine intolerance. Of course, manufacturers can decide to do a new and improved version so always check carefully!

Carob [Siesta D&D Chocolates Ltd]
Carob Powder (cocoa alternative) [Cotswold]
Cheddar style slices (Creamy & Smooth) [Tofutti]
Cornflakes [Kellogg's]
Custard Powder (Original) [Bird's]
Damson Stoneless Jam [Tiptree, Wilkin & Sons Ltd]
Hobnob biscuits [McVities]
Ice-Cream [Swedish Glace]
Organic chopped tomatoes (tinned) [Biona]
Organic stock cubes, chicken and vegetable [Kallo]
Pork sausages [Tesco Finest]
Quick yeast [Doves Farm]
Red Bush tea (naturally caffeine free)
Salami Milano [Tesco Finest]
Soy sauce [Kikkoman]
Soya Dessert (caramel and vanilla) [Provamel Alpro]
Soya Dream (single cream alternative) [Provamel]
Soya Milk [Alpro]
Soya soft cheese [Tofutti]
Soya Topping Cream (whipped cream alternative) [Soyatoo]
Sunflower or soya spreads [Pure]
Tomato ketchup [Heinz]
Vegetable fat [Trex]
White bread baked in store [Tesco]
Worcestershire sauce [Lea and Perrins]

Some supermarkets label foods with allergy warnings. Supermarkets such as Tesco, which now stock a large range of free-from products, are making it easier to quickly spot ingredients to be avoided. Also, if you speak to the bakery department of your local supermarket, they should be able to show you a list of ingredients for you to check for their bread and other products baked on site.

E Numbers

Products containing many E numbers can mean that milk or citrus products have been added. I therefore avoid foods with lots of E numbers, and when buying something new, check on the internet that the specific E numbers are safe. The following websites are useful for doing this:

www.vegsoc.org
www.curezone.com/foods/enumbers.asp

Here is a list of ingredients which should be avoided for milk intolerance. (Of course, there are more, but these are the most common ones.)

Bread (unless it says that it does not contain milk)
Butter or buttermilk
Casein (and other products beginning like casein e.g. caseinate)
Cheese (other than milk-free)
Cream
Lactose (and other products beginning like lactose e.g. lactalburnim)
Milk other than soya or rice (some people can tolerate sheep or goat's milk)
Rusks (unless it says that it does not contain milk)
Whey
Yoghurt (unless it says that it does not contain milk)

The following is a list of some ingredients to be avoided for a caffeine-free diet.

Chocolate / Cocoa
Coffee
Coke-a-Cola
Tea (even decaf is not completely caffeine-free)

The following is a list of some ingredients which should be avoided for citrus intolerance.

Brandy
Champagne
Citric acid
Citrons
Cooking and some green apples (sweet-red ones are alright)
Grapefruit
Green grapes (red ones are alright)
Lemon
Lime
Malic Acid
Mandarin
Orange
Pineapple
Satsuma
Tangerine
White wine (red is alright)

There are a number of websites dealing with milk (lactose), citrus and caffeine intolerance which can be accessed by a Google search. Also, health food shops can usually advise on suitable foods for your diet.

Lactose is the primary sugar found in milk. Digestion of lactose requires the enzyme lactase, which breaks lactose into simple sugars. When the intestine produces little or no lactase, milk sugar is not digested. New-born babies require high intestinal lactase levels for survival. Later in life though about two-thirds of all people lose the ability to produce lactase. Most of the people who keep producing it throughout adulthood are those of European ancestry but in other ethnic groups – Mexican, African, Asian and Native American – 75 to 100 percent of adults are lactose intolerant. Primary lactose intolerance may begin at any time but usually develops in early adolescence and continues through life. Lactose intolerance means avoiding foods such as cream, butter, yoghurt and ice-cream as well as many prepared foods to which lactose is added such as bread, cereal, salad dressings, cake mixes and frozen meals.

Citrus intolerance often seems to come along with a milk intolerance. Citrus products can irritate arthritis symptoms. Migraine sufferers are advised to avoid milk and caffeine. Professional singers cut back on milk as it encourages the body to produce mucus and so affects the voice. Athletes do the same to improve their breathing.

Eating out can be tricky, it is best to warn restaurants before you arrive about your special requirements. If you look on the internet, there are hotels and restaurants which specialise in meals for intolerance sufferers. Some of the food served at McDonalds is suitable for milk, citrus and caffeine-free diets. Their website: www. mcdonalds.co.uk lists all of the ingredients they use.

Some meals do not need altering to suit a milk-, citrus- and caffeine-free diet, so when eating out they are the best ones to choose. A roast dinner is fine as long as butter is not added to the vegetables and you ask how the gravy is made. Gammon and chips without a sauce will be suitable as is an English breakfast without sausage and black pudding. For dessert meringue with Summer fruits.

D&D Chocolates at: www.dandchocolates.com make milk-free chocolate and carob products in novelty shapes, e.g. Easter eggs and Christmas Tree hangings, ideal for presents for children.

Soups and Starters

Salad Niçoise

Recipes & Notes

Bacon and Tomato Soup

Delicious with crusty bread. Serves 3 to 4. Takes 30 mins.

2 tbsp (30ml) olive oil
1 onion, finely chopped
9 oz (250g) bacon cut into small pieces
1lb 5oz (600g) tomatoes
2 tbsp (30ml) tomato ketchup
¼ pt (140ml) water
Salt and pepper
2 tbsp (5g) chopped fresh parsley to garnish

1. Heat the oil in a large pan over a medium heat. Cook the onions and bacon, stirring occasionally, for 5 minutes or until the onions are soft and the bacon is browning.
2. To prepare the tomatoes, remove any stalks then cut a small cross on the opposite sides. Place in a deep heatproof bowl and pour boiling water over them. Leave for 1 minute or until the skins split. Drain and pour over plenty of cold water. Using a small sharp knife, remove the skins and chop. Or substitute tinned tomatoes.
3. Stir in the tomatoes, ketchup and water. Bring to the simmer and cook gently for 10-15 minutes.
4. Process with a blender or food processor and then pass through a fine sieve. Season to taste. If the soup is too thick reheat, adding extra water.
5. Pour into bowls and garnish with the fresh parsley.

NOTE: *It is easier to use tinned tomatoes, but they tend to contain lemon juice so only use if they are citrus-free or if you do not have a citrus intolerance. Also check that the tomato ketchup is citrus-free.*

Chicken and Mushroom Salad

Serves 4. Takes 35 mins.

3⅓ tbsps (50ml) olive oil
1 tbsp (15ml) honey
Salt and pepper
1 packet of mixed salad leaves
1 oz (28g) dairy-free margarine
4½ oz (130g) chicken cut into chunks
4½ oz (130g) mixed mushrooms

1. Mix the olive oil, honey and seasoning to make the dressing.
2. Put the salad leaves into a bowl and pour over the dressing. Toss until coated.
3. Melt the margarine in a frying pan. Cook the chicken until brown and crisp. Just before the chicken is cooked add the mushrooms and cook until softened.
4. Toss the chicken and mushrooms with the salad and serve whilst still warm.

NOTE: *A little Dijon mustard can be added to the dressing but make sure it is citrus- and milk-free.*

Cream of Mushroom Soup

This recipe can also be used as a sauce to serve with chicken.

Serves 3 to 4. Takes 40 mins.

2 oz (55g) dairy-free margarine
1 onion, finely chopped
8 oz (225g) mushrooms
1oz (28g) plain flour
1 pint (475ml) vegetable stock
Salt and pepper
Pinch of nutmeg
½ pt (280ml) soya milk

1. Melt the margarine in a saucepan, add the onion and fry gently for about 5 minutes or until soft.
2. Roughly chop 6 oz (175g) of the mushrooms, add to the pan and continue to cook for a few minutes until quite soft.
3. Stir in the flour and cook for a minute or two, stirring continuously, then gradually add the stock and bring to the boil. Season with salt and pepper and add the nutmeg. Cover the pan and simmer gently for 15-20 minutes or until tender.
4. Cool a little, and then rub the soup through a sieve. Return to a clean pan.
5. Finely chop the remaining mushrooms and add to the soup with the milk. Bring back to the boil and simmer gently for 5-10 minutes.

NOTE: *Freeze without adding the milk and then add once defrosted. Check that the stock cubes are free from citrus and milk products.*

Melon with Parma Ham

Serves 4. Takes 20 mins.

1 melon
3 oz (85g) Parma ham
3 oz (85g) raspberries
Icing sugar to taste

1. To make the raspberry coulis, puree the raspberries in a blender or food processor. Add the icing sugar to taste. Push through a sieve to remove the seeds.
2. Cut the melon into portions, display on a plate with the Parma ham and pour over the raspberry coulis.

NOTE: *Other fruits such as redcurrants can be used. The coulis can be frozen for later and served with ice-cream.*

Pasta with Bacon Sauce

This can also be eaten as a light lunch. Serves 4. Takes 35 mins.

12 oz (350g) dried pasta shapes
14 oz (400g) tomatoes
1 tbsp (15ml) tomato ketchup
Salt and pepper
8 oz (225g) rindless streaky bacon
4 tbsp (60ml) olive oil
4 tbsp (10g) chopped parsley

1. Cook the pasta in a large pan of boiling salted water for about 10 minutes.
2. To prepare the tomatoes, remove any stalks then cut a small cross on the opposite sides. Place in a deep heatproof bowl and pour boiling water over them. Leave for 1 minute or until the skins split. Drain and pour over plenty of cold water. Using a small sharp knife, remove the skins and chop. Or substitute with tinned tomatoes.
3. Meanwhile, roughly chop the bacon. Heat 2 tbsp (30ml) of the oil in a frying pan and fry the bacon until golden. Stir in the tomatoes, ketchup and herbs and heat through for 2-3 minutes until piping hot. Adjust the seasoning.
4. Drain the pasta and toss with the remaining oil. Add the bacon sauce and toss well. Leave covered for 1 minute, then toss again and serve immediately.

NOTE: *It is easier to use tinned tomatoes, but they often contain lemon juice and so only use if they are citrus-free. Make sure the tomato ketchup is citrus-free.*

Salad Niçoise

Also ideal for a light lunch, serve with French bread. Serves 4. Takes 25 mins.

6 oz (170g) small new potatoes, scrubbed
Salt and pepper
6 tbsp (90ml) olive oil
7 oz (200g) can of tuna, drained
8oz (225g) tomatoes
½ small cucumber
½ crisp lettuce
8 oz (225g) French beans (pre-cooked)
2 hard-boiled eggs, quartered
8 anchovy fillets, drained and halved
2 tbsp (5g) fresh chopped parsley

1. Cook the potatoes in boiling salted water until tender. Whisk the oil and seasoning. Drain the potatoes, halve and toss in the oil. Leave to cool.
2. Flake the tuna into large chunks. Quarter the tomatoes, slice the cucumber.
3. Put the lettuce in a bowl and top with the tuna, tomatoes, cucumber, beans, eggs, anchovies and potatoes. Sprinkle with parsley.

NOTE: *A mild mustard can be added to the oil, but check it is citrus and milk-free.*

Main Courses and Snacks

Shepherds Pie

Boeuf Bourguignon

Serves 4. Takes 2½ hrs.

4 oz (110g) chopped bacon
2 lbs (900g) braising steak or topside
1 oz (28g) dairy-free margarine
2 tbsp (30ml) oil
2 tbsp (12g) plain flour
salt and pepper
⅓ pt (190ml) beef stock
⅔ pt (375ml) red Burgundy wine
12 button onions, peeled
6 oz (175g) button mushrooms, sliced

1. Cut the meat into 1½ inch (4cm) pieces. Heat half the margarine and oil in a flame-proof casserole dish and fry the bacon for 5 minutes. Drain. Fry the meat in batches for about 8 minutes or until browned.
2. Return the bacon to the casserole dish. Stir in the flour and add the seasoning, stock and wine, then bring to the boil stirring. Cover and cook at 170°C (325°F) Gas Mark 3 for 1½ hours.
3. Meanwhile, heat remaining margarine and oil in a frying pan and sauté the onions for 10 minutes or until golden brown. Remove and then add the mushrooms to the pan and fry for 5 minutes. Add the mushrooms and onions to the casserole. Cook for a further 30 minutes or until the meat is tender. If the gravy begins to dry up, stir in a little boiling water.

NOTE: *Make sure the stock cube is dairy and citrus-free. Serve with your choice of vegetables.*

Brown Bread

This recipe makes a medium brown loaf. Takes 5 hrs.

Make in a bread machine or by hand.

½ tsp (3g) dried yeast
7 oz (200g) strong white-flour
7 oz (200g) strong wholemeal-flour
1 tbsp (12g) sugar
½ oz (15g) dairy-free margarine
1 tsp (5g) salt
½ pint (280ml) water

1. Add all the ingredients to a bread machine in the order above and follow the instructions for a medium whole wheat loaf. If making the bread by hand, sift the flour and salt into a bowl, add the margarine and rub in with your fingers.
2. Dissolve the sugar in the water and sprinkle the dried yeast over the top. Leave in a warm place for about 10 minutes or until a thick frothy layer has formed on the top.
3. Add the yeast liquid to the dry ingredients and mix to a firm elastic dough, using a palette knife.
4. Turn onto a lightly floured surface and knead the dough for about 10 minutes or until smooth and no longer sticky. To do this, you punch the dough down and away from you using the palm of your hand, then fold it over towards you, give a quarter turn and repeat.
5. Shape the dough into a ball, place in a large oiled floured bowl and cover with a damp cloth or piece of plastic cling film. Put to rise in a warm place for about an hour or until the dough springs back when lightly pressed with a floured finger.
6. Remove the dough from the bag, turn out onto a lightly floured surface and 'knock back' by kneading until it is smooth and even again and the air bubbles have been knocked out.
7. The dough is now ready for shaping. Grease a loaf tin 2lb (900g). Shape the dough to fit the tin by kneading and rolling to give a shape as wide as the tin and a little longer. Tuck the ends under and place evenly in the tin.
8. Lay a sheet of oiled polythene lightly over the loaf and put to rise in a warm place until the dough reaches the tops of the tin.
9. Bake in a very hot oven 230°C (450°F) Gas Mark 8, allowing about 35 minutes. When ready the loaf should be well risen and golden brown and sound hollow when the base of the loaf is tapped.

NOTE: *Some bread-machine recipes recommend adding vitamin C but this is not always citrus-free so it is best to omit it. Others suggest adding milk powder, the finished product is not altered by leaving this out.* (See picture, page seven.)

Chicken Pie

Serves 4. Takes 45 mins.

6 oz (170g) plain flour / Pinch of salt
1½ oz (40g) dairy-free margarine
1½ oz (40g) white vegetable-fat / 5 tbsp (75ml) water
14 oz (400g) chicken breast, chopped
3½ oz (100g) mushrooms, chopped
1 oz (28g) dairy-free margarine
¼ pint (140ml) of water / ¼ pint (140ml) of soya milk
1 vegetable stock cube / 2 tbsp (14g) plain flour

1. Sift the flour and salt into a bowl. Add the fats cut into small pieces and rub in, until the mixture resembles fine breadcrumbs.
2. Add sufficient water, to mix to a pliable dough using a round-bladed knife. Add 3 tbsp (45ml) first and then gradually the rest of the water as required.
3. Turn out onto a lightly floured flat surface and knead very lightly until evenly mixed. If time allows, wrap the pastry in foil and chill for 30 minutes.
4. Fry the chicken and mushrooms in the margarine for 5 minutes, remove the mushrooms. Finish cooking the chicken.
5. Mix the water, milk and stock cube and add to the chicken, boil and cook for 10 min.
6. Mix the 2 tbsp (14g) of plain flour with a little water to make a paste. Add to the liquid, boil and stir until thick. Add the mushrooms.
7. Pour the mixture into the oven proof dish. Roll out the pastry and use to cover the mixture. Bake for 10 minutes until golden brown at 220°C (425°F) Gas Mark 7.

NOTE: *Check the vegetable stock cube is citrus and milk-free. Why not make double the pastry recipe and freeze some for another time.*

Chicken Stir Fry with Vermicelli

Spaghetti can be used instead of vermicelli. Serves 4. Takes 25 mins.

10 oz (280g) chicken breast
6 oz (175g) dried vermicelli
3 tbsp (45ml) of soy sauce / 1 tbsp (15ml) of clear honey
1 inch (3cm) piece of fresh ginger / 2 carrots / 1 red pepper
4 oz (110g) mangetout / 4 oz (110g) baby sweet corn
3½ oz (100g) mushrooms / 1 tbsp (15ml) of sunflower oil
1 vegetable stock cube

1. Cut the light brown skin off the ginger. Cut the ginger into thin slices, and then cut the slices into very thin strips. Put the soy sauce and honey in a bowl. Add the pieces of ginger and stir them well.
2. Cut the chicken into strips, add to the marinade and stir well. If time leave for 30 mins.
3. Peel the carrots and cut them into thin sticks. Cut the ends off the pepper and chop in half and cut out the seeds. Slice into thin strips. Cut the stalks off the mangetout. Slice the top off the sweet corn and cut them into quarters. Slice the mushrooms.
4. Heat the oil in a frying pan. When hot, spoon in the chicken leaving the marinade in the bowl. Cook the chicken for about five minutes. Once the chicken is cooked add all the vegetables. Stir for three minutes.
5. Make up ½ pt (140ml) of stock, mix with the marinade and pour over the other ingredients. Let it boil and cook for two more minutes.
6. Cook the vermicelli as on the packet. Drain and add to the vegetables. Stir, leave for a minute and then serve.

NOTE: *Check the soy sauce is citrus-free. Check the vegetable stock cube is milk and citrus-free.*

Chicken with Honey and Soy Sauce

Serves 4. Takes 20 mins.

4 chicken breasts
2 tbsp (30ml) clear honey
2 tbsp (30ml) soy sauce
Sunflower oil

1. Cut the chicken into small pieces. Heat the oil in the frying pan.
2. Once hot, add the chicken and pour over the soy sauce.
3. Turn the chicken as it cooks, until browned and cooked through.
4. Add the honey and stir until lightly glazed, be careful it does not burn.
5. Serve with vegetables or pasta.

NOTE: *Check the soy sauce is citrus-free.*

Chicken with Tomato and Bacon

Serves 4. Takes 40 mins.

4 chicken breasts
4 rashers of back bacon
4 oz (110g) tomatoes
2 tbsp (30ml) tomato ketchup
Sunflower oil

1. Heat the oil in a saucepan. Wrap the bacon around the chicken and fry in the oil for about 30 minutes, making sure it is cooked through. Pour off any excess oil.
2. To prepare the tomatoes, remove any stalks then cut a small cross on the opposite sides. Place in a deep heatproof bowl and pour boiling water over them. Leave for 1 minute or until the skins split. Drain and pour over plenty of cold water. Using a small sharp knife, remove the skins and chop. Or substitute with citrus-free tinned tomatoes.
3. Mix the tomatoes and ketchup and pour over the chicken. Cook for a further 5 minutes.

NOTE: *Check the tomato ketchup does not contain lemon juice. It is easier to use tinned tomatoes, but most contain lemon juice so only use if they are citrus-free.*

Cod and Bacon with Green Beans

A quick and easy recipe. Serves 4. Takes 25 mins.

2 good handfuls of green beans
Salt and pepper
Olive oil
4 x 8 oz (225g) cod steaks, on the bone or cod loins
12 slices of streaky bacon, chopped
1 handful of pine nuts

1. Preheat the oven to 220°C (425°F) Gas Mark 7. Place the green beans in a roasting tin. Season with salt and pepper, add just enough olive oil to coat the beans and mix it around.
2. Nestle the cod steaks in among the beans, place the bacon over the cod and beans. Sprinkle the pine nuts over the top.
3. Lightly lay kitchen foil over the fish for the first 5 minutes of cooking. Remove the foil and cook for a further 10 minutes.

NOTE: *Of course, fish is traditionally served with lemon juice, so if you do not have a citrus intolerance add a lemon halved to the tray and cook with the fish.*

Creamy Chicken with Pasta

Serves 4. Takes 30 mins.

8 oz (225g) pasta
¾ oz (21g) dairy-free margarine
¾ oz (21g) plain flour
½ pint (280ml) soya milk/cream substitute (change the proportions,
depending how rich you like your sauce)
6 oz (170g) cooked chicken (smoked chicken adds to the flavour)
3½ oz (100g) mushrooms
salt and pepper
a little parsley

1. Cook the pasta in a large pan of fast-boiling water as instructed by the packet.
2. Make a white sauce by gently heating the dairy-free margarine, then stirring in the plain flour to make a paste. Cook for a couple of minutes and then slowly add the milk and cream stirring continuously. Use a whisk to avoid lumps.
3. Drain the pasta thoroughly and return to the saucepan with the white sauce, chopped chicken and thinly sliced mushrooms. Add salt and pepper to taste and stir until heated through.

NOTE: *Why not top with dairy-free cheese?*

Easy Chicken with Mushrooms

Serve with vegetables of your choice. Serves 4. Takes 35 mins.

14 oz (400g) skinless chicken breasts
7 oz (200g) mixed mushrooms, chopped
1½ oz (40g) dairy-free margarine
½ pint (280ml) chicken stock
1 handful of fresh thyme or a little dried thyme

1. Line a roasting tin with tinfoil, leaving two sides long enough to fold over the top.
2. Preheat the oven to 220°C (425°F) Gas Mark 7. Mix everything together in a bowl. Place inside the tinfoil with the stock. Close up the top of the tinfoil bag, making sure it is sealed and secure.
3. Place the roasting tin on a hob ring on a high heat for 1 minute to get the heat going, then bake in the middle of the oven for 25 minutes.
4. Meanwhile prepare the vegetables to serve with it.

NOTE: *Check that the chicken stock cube is citrus and milk-free.*

Honey Glazed Duck with Pears in Red Wine

Serves 4. Takes 1hr.

3 or 4 duckling breast fillets
Salt
2 tbsp (30ml) honey
2 large firm ripe pears
2 oz (55g) caster sugar
½ pint (280ml) of red wine

1. Prick the duckling breast skin all over with a skewer or fork and rub well with salt to help crisp the skin. Place, skin side up on a rack or trivet in a roasting tin.
2. Bake in the oven at 180°C (350°F) Gas Mark 4 for 15 minutes. Brush the skin with honey and cook for a further 15 minutes or until cooked through.
3. Meanwhile peel the pears. Put the sugar and wine in a saucepan just large enough to hold the pears and heat gently until the sugar has dissolved.
4. Add the pears to the wine, standing them upright in the pan. Cover and simmer gently for 20-35 minutes until the pears are just tender, basting them from time to time with the liquid.
5. Serve the duckling breasts with your choice of vegetables and add a pear topped with the wine sauce.

Mango and Chicken Pancakes

Serves 4. Takes 25 mins.

2 oz (55g) plain flour
Pinch of salt
1 egg
¼ pint (140ml) soya milk
Sunflower oil
1 egg
1 lb (450g) chicken, chopped
1 ripe mango, chopped into small pieces
2 tomatoes, sliced

1. Sift flour and salt into a bowl and make a well in the middle. Break the egg into the well and add about half of the liquid.
2. Gradually work the flour into the liquid using a hand whisk. Beat until smooth. Add the rest of the liquid, a little at a time, beating until smooth.
3. Heat a little oil in a frying pan, pour in a quarter of the liquid and cook on both sides, repeat making 4 pancakes. Wrap the pancakes in foil and keep warm under a low grill setting.
4. Meanwhile heat a little oil in a pan and cook the chicken thoroughly. Fold in the mango pieces. Divide the filling between the pancakes. Fold into neat squares and arrange on a foil-lined grill pan. Top each pancake with slices of tomato.
5. Heat through under the grill until the tomatoes are lightly cooked and the pancakes are hot.

Oven Fried Chicken Drumsticks

These oven cooked drumsticks make a healthy alternative to traditional fried chicken. Serves 4. Takes 1 hr.

8 chicken drumsticks, skinned
Salt and pepper
2 tbsp (12g) plain flour
¼ tsp (1¼g) cayenne pepper (optional)
2 egg whites, whisked lightly
3 oz (85g) fresh breadcrumbs (white or wholemeal)
2 tbsp (5g) fresh parsley
2 tbsp (30ml) olive oil
Salt and pepper

1. Season the chicken drumsticks with salt and pepper. Spread the flour on a plate, add the cayenne pepper if used and mix well. Spread the whisked egg whites on a second plate and the breadcrumbs on a third. Mix the parsley with the breadcrumbs.
2. Coat the drumsticks in the flour, then the egg white and then press on the breadcrumbs.
3. Preheat the oven to 190°C (375°F) Gas Mark 5. Heat the oil in a large frying pan until hot. Add the drumsticks and fry over a moderate heat, turning frequently, for about 5 minutes until golden on all sides.
4. Transfer the drumsticks to a baking tray and place in the oven for about 40 minutes or until the chicken feels tender when pierced with a skewer or fork. Turn from time to time to ensure they brown evenly.
5. Serve hot with chips etc.

NOTE: *Check that the bread is milk-free.*

Pan-Fried Pork Medallions with Parma Ham

Ideal for a special occasion. Serves 4. Takes 50 mins

14 oz (400g) pork fillet or 12 pork medallions of a similar weight
1 oz (28g) plain flour
1 egg, beaten with 2 tbsp (30ml) soya milk
5 oz (140g) breadcrumbs
2 oz (55g) dairy-free margarine
2 tbsp (30ml) sunflower oil
3 oz (85g) Parma ham
4 soya cheese slices, cut in half

1. Cut the pork fillet into 12 pieces and lightly beat the medallions using a rolling pin. Season the flour and coat each pork medallion evenly in flour, then in the egg and milk and finally in the breadcrumbs. If time place on a plate in a single layer, cover and chill until required. This stage can be prepared up to 24 hours in advance, but remove from the fridge 1 hour before cooking.
2. Preheat the oven to 190°C (375°F) Gas Mark 5. Melt half the margarine and oil in a frying pan and cook half the pork medallions for 4-5 minutes until golden on each side, turning occasionally. Keep warm in the oven while you cook the rest of the pork.
3. Layer the pork medallions in stacks of three, with the Parma ham and soya cheese slices and return to the oven for a further 2 minutes. Arrange on plates and serve with your choice of vegetables.

NOTE: *Check that the bread is milk-free.*

Pasta Carbonara

Serves 4. Takes 20 mins.

8-10 rashers of back bacon
3½ oz (100g) mushrooms
Sunflower oil
3 to 4 eggs, beaten
10 to 12 handfuls of pasta tubes
Salt and pepper and a little dried mixed herbs if you wish
1 oz (28g) dairy-free margarine
4 tbsp (60ml) soya cream-substitute

1. Fry the bacon and mushrooms in a little sunflower oil until browned. Pour off the left-over oil. Meanwhile boil the water and cook the pasta as instructed on the packet.
2. Whisk the eggs with the seasoning and add the margarine and soya cream. Drain the pasta and set to one side.
3. Cut up the bacon and return to the pan with the mushrooms and pasta. Pour the egg mixture over the top.
4. Stir together over the heat until the egg is cooked and has coated the other ingredients.
5. Serve immediately.

NOTE: *Why not top with a little soya cheese?*

Pizza

Serves 4. Takes 1hr 20 mins.

11 oz (310g) strong plain white flour
1 tsp (5g) salt / ½ tsp (3g) fast-action dried yeast
½ tbsp (6g) sugar / ½ oz (15g) dairy-free margarine
7½ fl oz (210ml) water / Tomato ketchup
Toppings of your choice

1. In a warm bowl, mix the flour, salt, yeast and sugar. Make a well in the centre and add the water and dairy-free margarine.
2. Stir the mixture by hand or with a wooden spoon until it forms a wet dough. Beat for a further 2-3 minutes. OR mix the ingredients in a bread making machine.
3. Turn out the dough on to a well floured surface and knead for about 5 minutes, or until smooth and elastic. Place in a bowl, cover and leave in a warm place until doubled in size, about 45 minutes.
4. Turn out the dough on to a floured surface and knead again for 2-3 minutes. Place a lightly oiled flat baking sheet in a hot oven at 220°C (425°F) Gas Mark 7 to heat.
5. Roll out the dough to a circle roughly 10 inch (25cm) diameter. Place on the heated baking sheet and press up the edges. Cover the dough with tomato ketchup and add the toppings of your choice, bake for 20 minutes.

NOTE: *Once made, the dough can be frozen and defrosted when required. Check the tomato ketchup is citrus-free. Topping ideas: mushrooms, tomatoes, peppers, bacon, ham, chicken, salami, pepperoni or tuna. It is possible to find milk and citrus-free salami and pepperoni in supermarkets.*

Of course pizza needs cheese, there are milk-free alternatives but with enough flavours on the pizza, cheese is not necessary.

Pork and Bacon Meatballs

Serves 4. Takes 45 mins.

1 small onion / 2 tbsp (30ml) olive oil / 2 garlic cloves, finely chopped
2 rashers streaky bacon, chopped / 14 oz (400g) pork mince
2 oz (55g) fresh white breadcrumbs
1 tbsp (2½g) finely chopped fresh sage or a little dried sage
14 oz (400g) tomatoes skinned and chopped
1 tbsp (15ml) tomato ketchup
12 oz (340g) dried spaghetti or other pasta / Salt and pepper

1. Finely chop and fry the onion in half the oil for 3 minutes, until soft. Add the garlic and bacon and cook for 3 minutes, stirring occasionally. Put the pork in a bowl with the bacon mix, breadcrumbs, sage and seasoning. Mix together and shape into 24 even-sized balls.
2. Fry the meatballs in the remaining oil in a large pan for 3-4 minutes, turning them often.
3. To prepare the tomatoes, remove any stalks then cut a small cross on the opposite sides. Place in a deep heatproof bowl and pour boiling water over them. Leave for 1 minute or until the skins split. Drain and pour over plenty of cold water. Using a small sharp knife, remove the skins and chop. Or substitute with citrus-free tinned tomatoes.
4. Add the tomatoes and ketchup to the frying pan. Cover with a lid and simmer for 10-15 minutes. Meanwhile, cook the pasta according to the pack instructions. Drain and divide between four warmed plates. Top with the meatballs and sauce.

NOTE: *Check the bread does not contain milk products. This dish can be topped with a little grated soya cheese. Make sure the tomato ketchup is citrus-free. It is easier to use tinned tomatoes, but they tend to contain lemon juice so only substitute if they are citrus-free.*

Pork, Apple and Stuffing Burgers

Makes 8 burgers. Takes 1 hr including chilling time.

1x lb 2oz (500g) pack, pork mince
1 small onion, finely chopped
1 red apple, finely chopped
3½ oz (85g) pack sage and onion stuffing mix
1 egg yolk
2 tbsp (30ml) olive oil plus extra for brushing
Salt and pepper
Burger buns

1. Break up the mince in a large bowl, and then add the other ingredients. Mix well, and season with salt and pepper.
2. Using wet hands, divide the mixture into eight evenly sized balls. Flatten into patties, approximately 3 inch (7½cm) diameter and 1 inch (2½ cm) thick. Chill in the fridge for at least 30 minutes or until ready to cook.
3. Preheat the oven to 180°C (350°F) Gas Mark 4. Brush the patties with oil and then cook in batches on a hot griddle for 2 minutes on each side. Transfer to the oven for a further 10 minutes until cooked through.
4. Serve in toasted buns with sliced tomato etc.

NOTE: *If you do not have a citrus intolerance, a cooking apple can be used instead.*

Quiche

Serves 4. Takes 1 hr.

6 oz (170g) plain flour
Pinch of salt
1½ oz (40g) dairy-free margarine
1½ oz (40g) white vegetable-fat
3 tbsp (45ml) water
(Or 1 pack of ready-made short crust pastry)
8 oz (225g) bacon, chopped
1¾ oz (50g) mushrooms
2 eggs, beaten
½ pint (280ml) soya milk
Salt and pepper
Pinch of ground nutmeg
Sliced tomato

1. Sift the flour and salt into a bowl. Add the fats cut into small pieces and rub in, until the mixture resembles fine breadcrumbs.
2. Add sufficient water to mix to a pliable dough, using a round-bladed knife. Add 3 tbsp (45ml) first and then gradually the rest of the water as required.
3. Turn out onto a lightly floured flat surface and knead very lightly until evenly mixed. If time allows, wrap the pastry in foil and chill for 30 minutes.
4. Preheat the oven to 220°C (425°) Gas Mark 7. Roll out the pastry and line an 8 inch (20cm) flan ring or dish. Cover with greaseproof paper and weight down with the pastry off cuts. Cook for 10 minutes, uncover and cook for another 5 minutes.
5. Fry the bacon in its own fat in a small saucepan with the mushrooms. Drain the bacon and mushrooms and add to the pastry case.
6. Beat the eggs with the soya milk and add the seasoning and nutmeg. Pour into the pastry case over the bacon and mushrooms. Top with sliced tomatoes.
7. Stand the quiche on a hot baking sheet and bake for 15 minutes, reduce the temperature to 180°C (350°F) Gas Mark 4 and continue to cook for 25 minutes or until the filling is set and golden brown.

NOTE: *Sausage, courgette, tuna and many other fillings can be added to quiche. Quiche usually contains cheese, with enough fillings it will not be missed. Otherwise, grate dairy-free cheese over the top.*

It is sometimes possible to find ready made short crust pastry which is milk-free. This will reduce the preparation time. (See picture, page three.)

Roasted Sea Bass

Good for special occasions, as sea bass can be expensive.

Serves 4. Takes 40 mins.

4 x 8 oz (225g) sea bass fillets
1 handful of mixed herbs
2 lb 3 oz (1kg) potatoes
Olive oil
Salt and pepper
2 knobs of dairy-free margarine
8 oz (225g) mixed mushrooms, sliced

1. Preheat the oven to 240°C (475°F) Gas Mark 9. Rub a baking tray with olive oil. Cut slits in the fish fillets about half-way down and stuff the cuts with herbs. Set to one side.
2. Slice the potatoes lengthways, ⅓ inch (just under 1cm) thick. Dry them off with kitchen paper and very lightly coat with olive oil. Season with salt and pepper, then lay them in the tray. Cook the potatoes in the oven for around 15 minutes until just cooked.
3. Meanwhile put the margarine into a pan and fry the mushrooms. Take the pan off the heat. Scatter the mushrooms over the potatoes. Place the sea bass fillets on top. Bake in the oven for 12-15 minutes.
4. Remove the tray from the oven, put some foil over the top and let it sit for about 5 minutes.

Salmon Fillet wrapped in Prosciutto

Serves 4. Takes 10 mins.

4 x 8 oz (225g) salmon fillets, skinned and pin-boned
Pepper
8 slices of prosciutto
Olive oil
4 handfuls of mixed salad leaves

1. Preheat the oven to 220°C (425°F) Gas Mark 7. Season the salmon with a little pepper before wrapping them in prosciutto slices. Leave some of the flesh exposed.
2. Drizzle with olive oil and roast in the oven for around 10 minutes until the prosciutto is golden.
3. Place the cooked fish on a bed of salad leaves and serve with your choice of vegetables.

Sausage and Potato Casserole

Serves 4, takes 50 mins.

8 large sausages
Sunflower oil
1 lb (450g) small new potatoes
3½ oz (100g) mushrooms
2 carrots
1 vegetable stock cube
4 tbsp (25g) plain flour

1. Heat the oil in a frying pan and cook the sausages. Meanwhile boil the potatoes. Add the mushrooms to the frying pan a few minutes before the sausages are cooked.
2. Chop the sausages into bite sized pieces and drain the potatoes. Place the sliced mushrooms, chopped carrots, sausages and potatoes into an oven proof dish with a lid. Preheat the oven to 200°C (400°F) Gas Mark 6.
3. Make up ½ pint (280ml) of stock and pour into the dish. Cover and put into the oven for about 20 minutes, stirring occasionally.
4. Mix the plain flour with a little water to make a paste. Add to the dish and stir well. Cook for a further 15 minutes or until the sauce has thickened.

NOTE: *Check the ingredients carefully for the sausages, making sure they are milk-free. Make sure the vegetable stock cubes are citrus and milk-free. Why not add other vegetables e.g. broccoli. This recipe is ideal to be made in advance and then just simmered until everyone is ready to eat.*

Sausage Pasta

This would be eaten every day in our house given the chance! Serves 4. Takes 40 mins.

3½ oz (100g) mushrooms / 1 tbsp (15ml) sunflower oil
8-10 large sausages
8 oz (225g) tomatoes, skinned and chopped
4 tbsp (60ml) tomato ketchup
10 good handfuls of pasta quills

1. Heat the oil in a large frying pan. Slice the mushrooms and arrange around the outside of the pan. Remove the skins from the sausages, by cutting them in half and forcing the meat out of the skins using a knife. This gives a better texture than just cutting up the sausages.
2. Put the sausage meat into the frying pan, cook on one side until browned. Put a pan of water onto boil. Turn the mushrooms and sausages and cook until browned on the other side. Cook the pasta quills as instructed on the pack.
3. Meanwhile to prepare the tomatoes, remove any stalks then cut a small cross on the opposite sides. Place in a deep heatproof bowl and pour boiling water over them. Leave for 1 minute or until the skins split. Drain and pour over plenty of cold water. Using a small sharp knife, remove the skins and chop. Or substitute with citrus-free tinned tomatoes.
4. Once the sausage is cooked through using a spatula break up into small pieces and mix with the mushrooms. Add the tomatoes and ketchup and stir until thoroughly mixed.
5. Drain the pasta and add to the sausage mixture. Stir well and serve immediately.

NOTE: *Check the ingredients on sausages very carefully for milk products. Make sure the tomato ketchup is citrus-free. It is easier to use tinned tomatoes, but they tend to contain lemon juice so only use if they are citrus-free.*

Sausage Rolls

This takes a long time to prepare, but sausage rolls are something you miss out on with a dairy-free diet. Why not make extra and freeze them for another time. Makes about 10 sausage rolls. Takes 35 mins, plus 2 hrs if making your own pastry.

8 oz (225g) plain flour
½ tsp (2½g) salt
3 oz (85g) dairy-free margarine
3 oz (85g) white vegetable fat
¼ pt (140ml) iced water
(Or 1 pack of Puff or Flaky pastry)
1 lb (450g) sausage meat
1 small onion / Salt and pepper
Beaten egg to glaze

1. If not using ready made pastry, sift the flour and salt into a bowl and rub in a quarter of both fats until the mixture resembles breadcrumbs. Add sufficient water to the dry ingredients to mix to a fairly soft elastic dough. Knead lightly on a floured surface and roll out to a strip 3 times as long as it is wide.
2. Divide the remaining fat into three equal portions and use one part to cut into small flakes which should be laid evenly over the top two-thirds of the pastry.
3. Fold the bottom third of the pastry upwards, and the top third downwards, seal the edges and squash the open edges with the rolling pin. Put into a polythene bag and chill in the fridge for 20 minutes.
4. Remove the pastry from the fridge and with the folded side of the pastry to the right, roll out again to a strip three times as long as it is wide. Repeat the flaking process with the second portion of fat, fold up as before and wrap and chill again for 20 minutes.
5. Repeat step 4 using the final portion of fat and chill for 15 minutes. A final rolling and folding process may be carried out without adding any fat. Chill the pastry for an hour and it is ready for use.
6. Combine the sausage meat, onion and seasonings. Divide the sausage meat into four and roll each into a long sausage about 10 inch (about 25cm) long.
7. Roll out the pastry thinly and cut into two squares of about 10 inches (about 25cm), then cut each square into two strips of 10 x 5 inches (25 x 12½cm).
8. Lay one roll of sausage meat on each piece of pastry keeping it to one side of the centre. Damp the edges of pastry and fold over to enclose the filling. Press the edges firmly together and flake with a sharp knife. Cut into about 8 or 10 pieces. Place on lightly greased or dampened baking sheets.
9. Glaze each one with beaten egg and make two or three cuts along the top, depending on size. Bake in a hot oven 220°C (425°F) Gas Mark 7 for about 25-30 minutes, or until well puffed up and golden brown.

NOTE: *It is sometimes possible to find flaky or puff pastry ready made which does not contain milk, but check the ingredients. Also check the ingredients of the sausage meat. (See picture, page one.)*

Shepherds Pie

Although this dish takes a long time to cook and prepare it is worth doubling the recipe and freezing one for another time. Freeze after covering with mashed potato and make sure it is completely defrosted before cooking.

Serves 4. Takes 1 hr 10 mins.

1½ lb (680g) potatoes
1 oz (28g) dairy-free margarine
2 tbsp (30ml) soya milk
Salt and pepper
1tbsp (15ml) sunflower oil
1 large onion, finely chopped
1½ lb (680g) lamb mince
2 carrots, finely chopped
2 tbsp (12g) plain flour
8 fl oz (225ml) vegetable stock
30ml (2tbsp) Worcestershire sauce
4 oz (110g) frozen peas

1. Peel the potatoes and cut into chunks. Cook in a large pan of boiling water for 15-20 minutes, or until tender. Drain the potato well and return to the pan over low heat, and stir to evaporate any excess water. Remove from the heat, add the margarine and soya milk, and mash the potato until smooth. Season with salt and pepper. Preheat the oven to 180°C (350°F) Gas Mark 4.
2. Meanwhile, heat the oil in a large frying pan and add the onion. Cook, stirring occasionally, until soft and just beginning to colour. Add the mince, increase the heat and cook until browned, breaking up any lumps with a wooden spoon as the meat cooks. Drain off the excess oil.
3. Add the carrots to the pan and cook for a few minutes until just tender. Sprinkle on the flour and cook, stirring for 1 minute. Slowly add the stock, stirring constantly. Add the Worcestershire sauce. Bring to the boil and cook for 2-3 minutes, or until the gravy thickens. Season to taste with salt and pepper. Stir in the peas and transfer the mixture to a 4¼ pint (2 litre) ovenproof dish.
4. Spoon the mashed potato onto the meat mixture and spread out evenly. Use a fork to swirl the surface. Bake for 40-50 minutes, or until the potato is golden.

NOTE: *Make sure the vegetable stock cube is citrus and milk-free. Check the ingredients on the Worcestershire sauce. (See picture, page nineteen.)*

Speedy Coq au Vin

Serves 4. Takes 25 mins.

1 lb (450g) chicken breast, cubed
4 oz (110g) bacon, chopped
7 oz (200g) mushrooms
1 pt (450ml) chicken stock
¼ pt (140ml) red wine
2 tsp (10ml) Worcestershire sauce
Salt and pepper
1 tbsp (2½g) chopped fresh thyme
1 tbsp (14g) flour

1. Dry-fry the chicken and the bacon in a saucepan for 5 minutes, stirring frequently.
2. Add the mushrooms to the chicken, with a couple of tablespoons of stock. Cook briskly for 2 minutes, then reduce the heat and pour on the remaining stock and wine.
3. Stir in the Worcestershire sauce, thyme and seasoning, to taste. Cover and simmer for 15 minutes. If the liquid does not thicken sufficiently, mix 1 tbsp (14g) of flour with a little water to make a paste. Slowly add this to the liquid stirring until it thickens.

NOTE: *Check the chicken stock cube is milk- and citrus-free. Also check that the Worcestershire sauce is citrus-free.*

Spicy Sausage and Mixed Wild Mushrooms

Serves 4. Takes 25 mins

1 onion, peeled and finely chopped
1 clove of garlic, peeled and finely chopped
9 oz (250g) spicy sausages, meat removed from the skins
1 tbsp (15ml) olive oil
1 handful of fresh thyme leaves picked, or a little dried thyme
14 oz (400g) mixed wild mushrooms, chopped
10 handfuls of pasta
Salt and pepper
3 good knobs of dairy-free margarine

1. Fry the onion, garlic and sausage meat in a little olive oil until lightly golden. Add the thyme and mushrooms. Continue to fry, cooking away any moisture from the mushrooms.
2. Meanwhile cook the pasta according to the instructions on the packet. Reserve a little cooking water.
3. Remove the sausage mixture from the heat, season to taste and loosen with the margarine and a little cooking water from the pasta.
4. Toss the drained pasta with the other ingredients.

NOTE: *Check the ingredients are milk-free for the sausages, if you cannot find spicy sausages, any will do just as well. This recipe is also good with a little grated soya cheese over the top.*

Stir-Fried Beef

Serves 4. Takes 30 mins

1 ¼ lb (570g) rump steak
1 garlic clove, crushed
4 tbsp (60ml) soy sauce / 4 tbsp (60ml) sunflower oil
½ oz (14g) fresh root ginger / Pepper
4 oz (110g) baby sweet corn / 6 oz (170g) mangetouts
4 oz (110g) mushrooms / 6 oz (170g) broccoli
3-4 fl oz (80-110ml) vegetable stock

1. Cut the steak into thin strips.
2. In a bowl, whisk the soy sauce with 2 tbsp (30ml) oil and the garlic. Peel and finely chop the ginger, stir into the bowl.
3. Add the beef to the bowl with plenty of pepper. If time cover and refrigerate, preferably over night.
4. Slice the corn cobs lengthwise into fine strips. Top and tail the mangetouts and thinly slice the mushrooms.
5. Divide the broccoli into small florets, trim the stalks and slice lengthwise into thin pieces. Cook the baby corn and broccoli for about 1 minute in boiling water and drain thoroughly.
6. Heat 2 tbsp (30ml) oil in a large frying pan or wok. Add the beef and marinade and cook through on a high heat for 2-3 minutes. Add the vegetables and stir-fry until warmed through.
7. Add the stock and allow to bubble up. Serve immediately with noodles.

NOTE: *Check the soy sauce is citrus-free. Check that the vegetable stock cube does not contain milk or citrus products.*

Toad in the Hole

Serves 4. Takes 35 mins, plus 30 mins to chill the batter if time allows.

4 oz (110g) plain flour
Pinch of salt
2 eggs
½ pt (280ml) soya milk
8 large sausages
2 tbsp (30ml) sunflower oil

1. Sift the flour and salt into a large bowl and make a well in the centre. Combine the eggs with the milk, and gradually add to the flour, whisking constantly until the batter is smooth. If time, cover and leave the batter in the fridge for 30 minutes.
2. Preheat the oven to 220°C (425°F) Gas Mark 7. Fry the sausages in 1 tbsp (15ml) of the oil until well browned all over, but not cooked through. Remove from the pan and set aside. Put the rest of the oil in an ovenproof dish and heat in the oven until smoking.
3. When the oil is hot, pour in the batter and add the sausages, spacing them out well. Bake for 20 minutes, or until the batter is well risen and browned. Serve with gravy and mashed potato.

NOTE: *Sausages often contain milk products, so read the ingredients very carefully.*

Turkey and Bacon Burgers

Makes 6. Takes 30 mins.

4 rashers back bacon
½ small red onion
1 slice brown bread
14 oz (400g) turkey mince
1 egg
Salt, pepper and parsley
Oil

1. Chop the bacon into small pieces and finely chop the onion.
2. Put the bread in a blender to make breadcrumbs.
3. Put the turkey mince in a large bowl and combine with the bacon, onion and bread.
4. Beat the egg and stir into the mixture. Season to taste with the salt, pepper and parsley and mix thoroughly.
5. Take handfuls of the mixture and form into six burger shapes.
6. Fry the burgers in a little oil, only turn them when you can see it is cooked half way through at the edge. This prevents the burger from falling apart in the frying pan.

Turkey Steaks

Serves 4. Takes 20 mins

4 turkey steaks
1 egg, beaten
2 oz (55g) plain flour
3 oz (80g) white breadcrumbs
Sunflower oil
Salt and pepper

1. Put the egg on one plate, the plain flour on another and the breadcrumbs mixed with the salt and pepper on a third.
2. Coat the steaks in the flour, then the egg and then the breadcrumbs.
3. Fry for about 10-15 minutes in the sunflower oil.
4. Serve with chips etc.

NOTE: *Check that the bread is milk-free.*

White Bread

This recipe can be made in a bread machine or by hand.

Nothing smells and tastes better than fresh home made bread.

Makes a medium white loaf. Takes 4 hrs.

½ tsp (3g) dried yeast
14 oz (400g) strong white flour
1 tbsp (15g) sugar
½ oz (14g) dairy-free margarine
1 tsp (5g) salt
9 fl oz (250ml) water

1. Add all the ingredients to a bread machine in the order above and follow the instructions for a medium white loaf. If making the bread by hand, sift the flour and salt into a bowl, add the margarine and rub in with your fingers.
2. Dissolve the sugar in the water and sprinkle the dried yeast over the top. Leave in a warm place for about 10 minutes or until a thick frothy layer has formed on the top.
3. Add the yeast liquid to the dry ingredients and mix to a firm, elastic dough, using a palette knife.
4. Turn onto a lightly floured surface and knead the dough for about 10 minutes or until smooth and no longer sticky. To do this, you punch the dough down and away from you using the palm of your hand, then fold it over towards you, give a quarter turn and repeat.
5. Shape the dough into a ball, place in a large oiled floured bowl and cover with a damp cloth or piece of plastic cling film. Put to rise in a warm place for about an hour or until the dough springs back when lightly pressed with a floured finger.
6. Turn out the dough onto a lightly floured surface and 'knock back' by kneading until it is smooth and even again and the air bubbles have been knocked out.
7. The dough is now ready for shaping. Grease a 2 lb (900g) loaf tin. Shape the dough to fit the tin by kneading and rolling to give a shape as wide as the tin and a little longer. Tuck the ends under and place evenly in the tin.
8. Lay a sheet of oiled polythene lightly over the loaf and put to rise in a warm place until the dough reaches the tops of the tins.
9. Bake in a very hot oven 230°C (450°F) Gas Mark 8, allowing about 35 minutes. When ready the loaf should be well risen and golden brown and sound hollow when the base of the loaf is tapped.

NOTE: *Some bread machine recipes suggest adding milk powder, but it does not affect the finished product to omit this. (See picture, page ten)*

Biscuits

Marbled Brownies

Recipes & Notes

Almond Topped Squares

Makes 18. Takes 50 mins.

3 oz (85g) dairy-free margarine
2 oz (55g) granulated sugar
1 egg yolk
½ tsp (2½ ml) vanilla essence
2 tbsp (30ml) soya cream, whipped
4 oz (110g) plain flour
For the topping:
4 egg whites
8 oz (225g) granulated sugar / 3 oz (85g) sliced almonds
½ tsp (2½g) ground ginger / ½ tsp (2½g) ground cinnamon

1. Preheat the oven to 190°C (375°F) Gas Mark 5. Line a 13 x 19 inch (33 x 48cm), or smaller swiss roll tin with greaseproof paper then grease the paper.
2. Cream the margarine and sugar until light and fluffy. Beat in the egg yolk, vanilla essence and soya cream.
3. Gradually stir in the flour. Press the dough into the prepared tin. Bake for 15 minutes. Remove from the oven but leave the oven on.
4. To make the topping, combine all the ingredients in a heavy saucepan. Cook stirring until the mixture comes to the boil. Boil for 1 minute. Pour over the dough, spreading evenly.
5. Return to the oven and bake for 15 to 20 minutes. Remove and leave to cool.

NOTE: *Most health food shops sell soya cream alternatives. Why not make Brittany cookies with the leftover egg yolks.*

Black Forest Brownies

Makes 16. Takes 45 mins.

3 oz (85g) plain flour
½ tsp (2½g) baking powder
4 oz (110g) dairy-free margarine
2 oz (55g) carob powder
2 eggs
6 oz (170g) caster sugar
1 tsp (5ml) vanilla extract
½ tsp (2½ml) almond extract
5 oz (150g) cherries, stones removed

1. Preheat the oven to 180°C (350°F) Gas Mark 4. Grease an 8 inch (20cm) square tin.
2. Sift together the flour and baking powder.
3. Place the margarine in a large saucepan over a medium heat and stir until melted. Remove from the heat and allow to cool a little, before adding the carob powder and stirring until smooth.
4. Beat in the eggs, sugar, vanilla and almond extracts.
5. Fold in the flour mixture and cherries. Pour into the tin and bake for about 20 minutes, or until just firm to the touch.
6. Cool in the tin, before cutting into squares.

NOTE: *If you cut the brownie into larger pieces it can be served as a pudding with a soya cream-substitute.*

Brittany Cookies

This is a richer version of shortbread. If you have egg yolks leftover from another recipe, this is an ideal way to use them up. Makes about 20. Takes 30 mins.

6 egg yolks, lightly beaten
1 tbsp (15ml) soya milk
9 oz (255g) plain flour
6 oz (170g) caster sugar
7 oz (200g) dairy-free margarine

1. Preheat the oven to 180°C (350°F) Gas Mark 4. Grease a heavy baking sheet. Mix 1 tbsp (15ml) of the egg yolks with the soya milk to make a glaze.
2. Sift the flour into a bowl. Add the egg yolks, sugar and margarine, and work them together until creamy.
3. Gradually bring in a little flour at a time until it forms a slightly sticky dough.
4. Using floured hands, pat out the dough to about ¼ inch (6mm) thick and cut out rounds using a 3 inch (7½cm) cutter. Transfer the rounds to the prepared baking sheet, brush each with a little egg glaze, then using the back of a knife, score with lines to create a lattice pattern.
5. Bake for about 12-15 minutes, until golden. Cool in the tin on a wire rack for 15 minutes, and then carefully remove the biscuits and leave to cool completely on the rack.

Butterscotch Meringue Bars

These are always eaten very quickly. Makes about 12. Takes 50 mins.

2 oz (55g) dairy-free margarine
6 oz (170g) dark brown sugar
1 egg
½ tsp (2½ml) vanilla essence
2 oz (55g) plain flour
Pinch of salt
¼ tsp (0.6g) grated nutmeg
For the topping:
1 egg white
Pinch of salt
1 tbsp (15ml) golden syrup
4 oz (110g) granulated sugar

1. Combine the margarine and brown sugar in a saucepan and cook until bubbling. Set aside to cool.
2. Preheat the oven to 180°C (350°F) Gas Mark 4. Line an 8 inch (20cm) square cake tin with greaseproof paper then grease the paper.
3. Beat the egg and vanilla essence into the cooled sugar mixture. Sift over the flour, salt and nutmeg and fold in. Spread over the bottom of the prepared cake tin.
4. To make the topping, beat the egg white with the salt until it holds soft peaks. Beat in the golden syrup, then the sugar and continue beating until the mixture holds stiff peaks.
5. Spread on the top of the mixture in the tin. Bake for 30 minutes. Cut into bars when cool.

Carob Cookies

Why not crumble one of these cookies over ice cream!

Makes 20. Takes 30 mins.

4 oz (110g) dairy-free margarine
4 oz (110g) light muscovado sugar
1 egg
1 tsp (5ml) vanilla essence
5 oz (140g) self-raising flour
3 oz (85g) porridge oats
3 oz (85g) carob, roughly chopped

1. Preheat the oven to 190°C (375°F) Gas Mark 5. Lightly grease two baking sheets. Cream the margarine with the sugar in a bowl until pale and fluffy. Add the egg and vanilla essence and beat well.
2. Sift the flour over the mixture and fold in lightly with a metal spoon, then add the oats and chopped carob and stir until evenly mixed.
3. Place small spoonfuls of the mixture in about 20 rocky heaps on the prepared baking sheets, leaving space for spreading.
4. Bake for 15-20 minutes, until beginning to turn pale golden. Cool for 2-3 minutes on the baking sheets, then transfer to wire racks to cool completely.

Carob Nest Cookies

Makes 20. Takes 45 mins.

6 oz (170g) carob
3½ oz (100g) dairy-free margarine
2 oz (55g) caster sugar
5 oz (140g) plain flour
1 egg, separated
3-4 oz (85-110g) desiccated coconut

1. Preheat the oven to 180°C (350°F) Gas Mark 4. Lightly grease 2 baking trays.
2. Melt one third of the carob in a small bowl set over a saucepan of simmering water. Add the margarine and heat until melted. Add the caster sugar and flour.
3. Separate the egg and put the white into a small bowl and the yolk into the bowl with the other ingredients.
4. Beat everything together until combined. Then using your hands shape the mixture into 20 even sized balls.
5. Put the coconut on a plate. Dip the balls first in the egg white, then in the coconut and roll them until they are evenly coated. Set 10 on each baking tray, then using your finger, make a deep print in the centre of each one to form the "nest".
6. Cook in the oven for 20 minutes then transfer to a cooling rack. Melt the rest of the carob and spoon a little into each "nest". Leave to set hard.

Carob Peppermint Crisps

Why not serve these with ice-cream. Makes 30.

Takes 25 mins and 45 mins for cooling.

2 oz (55g) granulated sugar
2 fl oz (55ml) water
1 tsp (5ml) peppermint essence
8 oz (225g) carob, chopped
oil

1. Lightly brush a large baking sheet with unflavoured oil. In a saucepan over a medium heat, heat the sugar and water, swirling the pan gently until the sugar dissolves. Boil rapidly to 138°C (280°F) on a sugar thermometer. If you don't have a sugar thermometer, test cooked sugar by spooning a few drops into a bowl of cold water, it should form a hard ball when rolled between your fingers. Be careful it does not turn brown and burn.
2. Remove the pan from the heat and add the peppermint essence, swirl to mix. Pour on to the prepared baking sheet and leave to set and cool completely, it will turn white.
3. When cold, break into pieces. Place in a food processor fitted with a metal blade and process to fine crumbs, do not over process.
4. Line two baking sheets with non-stick baking paper. Place the carob in a heatproof bowl over a saucepan of hot water. On a low heat stir frequently until the carob has melted and is smooth. Remove from the heat and stir in the peppermint mixture.
5. Using a teaspoon, drop small mounds on to the prepared sheets. Using the back of a spoon, spread to 1½ inch (4cm) rounds. Cool, then refrigerate for about 45 minutes, until set. Peel off the paper and store in an airtight container with non-stick baking paper between the layers.

Carob Tipped Cookies

If you do not have a piping bag, shape the dough with two teaspoons.

Makes 22. Takes 35 mins.

4 oz (110g) dairy-free margarine
3 tbsp (25g) icing sugar
5 oz (140g) plain flour
Few drops of vanilla essence
3 oz (85g) carob

1. Preheat the oven to 180°C (350°F) Gas Mark 4. Lightly grease two baking sheets. Put the dairy-free margarine and icing sugar in a bowl and cream together until very soft. Mix in the flour and vanilla essence.
2. Spoon the mixture into a large piping bag fitted with a large star nozzle and pipe lines on the prepared baking sheets. Cook for 15-20 minutes, until pale golden brown.
3. Leave to cool slightly before lifting on to a wire rack. Leave the biscuits to cool completely.
4. Put the carob in a small heatproof bowl. Stand in a saucepan of hot, not boiling water and leave to melt. Dip one end of each biscuit into the carob, put back on the rack and leave to set. Why not serve with a hot drink?

Coconut Oat Cookies

Makes 36. Takes 25 mins.

6 oz (170g) porridge oats
3 oz (85g) desiccated coconut
8 oz (225g) dairy-free margarine
4 oz (110g) granulated sugar
3 oz (85g) dark brown sugar
2 eggs
4 tbsp (60ml) soya milk
1½ tsp (7½ml) vanilla essence
4 oz (110g) plain flour
½ tsp (2g) bicarbonate of soda
Pinch of salt
1 tsp (2½ g) ground cinnamon

1. Preheat the oven to 200°C (400°F) Gas Mark 6. Lightly grease two baking sheets.
2. Spread the oats and coconut on an ungreased baking sheet. Bake for about 8 minutes until golden brown, stirring occasionally. Be careful they don't burn.
3. Cream the margarine and both kinds of sugar until light and fluffy. Beat in the eggs, one at a time, then add the soya milk and vanilla essence. Sift over the dry ingredients and fold in. Stir in the oats and coconut.
4. Drop spoonfuls of the dough leaving room for spreading on the baking sheets. Bake for 8-10 minutes. Transfer to a wire rack to cool.

Crunchy Oat Cookies

Makes 14. Takes 45 mins, including chilling time.

6 oz (170g) dairy-free margarine
4¼ oz (120g) caster sugar
1 egg yolk
6 oz (170g) plain flour
1 tsp (4g) bicarbonate of soda
Pinch of salt
1½ oz (42g) porridge oats
1½ oz (42g) cornflakes

1. Cream the margarine and sugar together until light and fluffy. Mix in the egg yolk.
2. Sift over the flour, bicarbonate of soda and salt and stir into the margarine mixture. Add the oats and cornflakes and stir to blend. Chill for at least 20 minutes.
3. Preheat the oven to 190°C (375°F) Gas Mark 5. Grease a baking sheet. Flour the bottom of a glass.
4. Roll the dough into balls using your hands. Place them on the prepared baking sheet and flatten with the bottom of the glass.
5. Bake for 10-12 minutes until golden. With a metal spatula, transfer to a wire rack to cool completely.

NOTE: *For nutty oat cookies, substitute the cornflakes for walnuts or pecans. Why not use the leftover egg white to make meringues?*

Date Crunch Cookies

Makes 24. Takes 25 mins, plus 1 hr 20 mins cooling time.

8 oz (225g) digestive biscuits
3 oz (85g) dairy-free margarine
2 tbsp (30ml) golden syrup
3 oz (85g) stoned dates, finely chopped
5 oz (140g) carob

1. Line a 7 inch (18cm) square shallow cake tin with foil. Put the biscuits in a plastic bag and crush roughly with a rolling pin.
2. Heat the margarine and golden syrup in a small saucepan until the margarine has melted.
3. Stir in the crushed biscuits and dates and mix well. Press the mixture into the prepared tin and chill for 1 hour.
4. Melt the chocolate in a bowl over a saucepan of hot water. Spread over the cookie mixture and chill until set.
5. Lift the foil out of the cake tin and peel away. Cut into 24 pieces.

Flapjacks

Makes 15. Takes 40 mins.

6 oz (170g) dairy-free margarine
3oz (85g) demerara sugar
75g (3oz) golden syrup
9 oz (255g) porridge oats
Pinch of salt

1. Preheat the oven to 180°C (350°F) Gas Mark 4. Line a deep 11 x 17 inch (28 x 42cm) tin with baking paper.
2. Place the margarine, sugar and golden syrup in a pan and heat gently until the margarine has melted. Stir in the porridge oats and a pinch of salt, then press the mixture down evenly into the tin.
3. Cook for about 25 minutes or until golden brown.
4. Mark into squares with a sharp knife, then leave to go completely cold before cutting-up.

NOTE: *3 oz (85g) glace cherries make a tasty addition, but as they usually contain lemon juice, dried papaya chunks can be used instead.*

Ginger Biscuits

Makes 20. Takes 30 mins.

4 oz (110g) dairy-free margarine
4 oz (110g) demerara sugar
1 tbsp (15ml) golden syrup
1 egg yolk
6 oz (170g) self-raising flour
1 tsp (2½g) ground ginger
1 tsp (5ml) water

1. Preheat the oven to 180°C (350°F) Gas Mark 4. Sprinkle two large baking sheets with flour.
2. Cream the margarine and sugar together until light and fluffy. Beat in the egg yolk and golden syrup.
3. Sieve the flour and ground ginger over the mixture. Gently fold in using a metal spoon for preference. If the mixture seems very dry and will not combine add the water.
4. Put walnut sized balls of the mixture onto the baking sheets leaving room for them to double in size. Press each one with the back of a fork dipped in flour.
5. Cook for about 12 minutes, check how quickly the biscuits are browning, return to the oven for another 5 minutes or until golden brown.
6. Leave to cool on the baking sheets for a few minutes, before transferring to a cooling rack.

Jam Meringue Bars

Makes 16. Takes 40 mins.

2 oz (55g) plain flour
2 oz (55g) dairy-free margarine
½ tsp (2½ml) vanilla essence
Pinch of salt
1 egg, separated
4 oz (110g) caster sugar
4 oz (110g) jam, e.g. strawberry

1. Preheat the oven to 180°C (350°F) Gas Mark 4. Grease a 9 inch (22cm) square baking tin. Beat together the flour, margarine, vanilla essence, salt, egg yolk and 2 oz (55g) of the sugar. Spread the mixture evenly over the base of the baking tin, prick it all over with a fork and bake in the oven for 10 minutes.
2. Beat the egg white until stiff. Gradually beat in the remaining 2 oz (55g) of the sugar until the mixture is smooth and glossy.
3. Remove the tin from the oven, spread the jam over the base and spread the meringue mixture to cover it evenly.
4. Bake in the oven for 20 minutes, until the meringue is crisp and light brown. Cool on a wire rack, and then cut into bars for serving.

NOTE: *It can be difficult to find jam which does not contain citrus products. If you make your own, just omit the lemon juice. The jam can be slightly runny though.*

Macadamia Caramel Squares

Makes 20. Takes 45 mins.

4 oz (110g) macadamia nuts
10 oz (300g) plain flour
6 oz (175g) soft brown sugar
4 oz (120g) dairy-free margarine
For the topping:
4 oz (110g) dairy-free margarine
3½ oz (100g) soft brown sugar
7 oz (200g) carob, chopped into small pieces

1. Preheat the oven to 180°C (350°F) Gas Mark 4. Coarsely chop the macadamia nuts.
2. To make the base, rub together the flour, sugar and margarine until the mixture resembles fine breadcrumbs.
3. Press the mixture into the bottom of a lined 8 inch (20cm) square tin. Sprinkle over the macadamia nuts.
4. To make the topping, put the margarine and sugar in a saucepan and stirring constantly bring the mixture to the boil.
5. Boil for 1 minute, stirring constantly. Pour the mixture over the macadamia nuts.
6. Bake for about 20 minutes, until the caramel topping is bubbling.
7. Remove from the oven and immediately sprinkle the carob pieces over the top. Leave for about 2 minutes, until the carob is beginning to melt and using the blade of a knife spread evenly over the top.
8. Leave to cool in the tin then cut into squares.

Macaroons

Makes 12. Takes 30 mins.

4 oz (110g) blanched almonds, toasted
5½ oz (155g) caster sugar
2 egg whites
½ tsp (2½ml) almond or vanilla essence
Icing sugar for dusting

1. Preheat the oven to 180°C (350°F) Gas Mark 4. Spread the almonds over a baking sheet and toast in the oven for about 10 minutes, make sure they do not burn.
2. Line a large baking sheet with non-stick baking paper. Reserve 12 almonds for decorating. In a food processor grind the rest of the almonds with the sugar.
3. With the machine running, slowly pour in enough of the egg whites to form a soft dough. Add the almond or vanilla essence and pulse to mix.
4. With moistened hands, shape the mixture into walnut sized balls and arrange on the baking sheet.
5. Press one of the reserved almonds on to each ball, flattening them slightly, and dust lightly with icing sugar. Bake for about 10-12 minutes, until the tops are golden and feel slightly firm. Transfer to a wire rack, cool slightly, and then peel the biscuits off the paper and leave to cool completely.

Marbled Brownies

Makes 24. Takes 1 hr, but well worth it.

8 oz (225g) carob
3 oz (85g) dairy-free margarine
4 eggs
12 oz (340g) caster sugar
4 oz (110g) plain flour
Pinch of salt
1 tsp (4g) baking powder
2 tsp (10ml) vanilla essence
For the plain batter:
2 oz (55g) dairy-free margarine
6 oz (170g) dairy-free soft cheese
4 oz (110g) caster sugar
2 eggs
2 tbsp (15g) plain flour
1 tsp (5ml) vanilla essence

1. Preheat the oven to 180°C (350°F) Gas Mark 4. Line a 13 x 9 inch (33 x 23cm) tin with greaseproof paper and grease the paper.
2. Melt the carob and margarine in a saucepan over a very low heat.
3. Meanwhile, beat the eggs until light and fluffy. Gradually add the sugar and continue beating until blended. Sift over the flour, salt and baking powder and fold in.
4. Stir in the cooled carob mixture and the vanilla essence. Once combined set aside 16 fl oz (475ml) of the carob batter.
5. To make the plain batter, cream the margarine and cream cheese with an electric mixer.
6. Add the sugar and continue beating until blended. Beat in the eggs, flour and vanilla essence.
7. Spread the unmeasured carob batter into the tin. Pour over the cream cheese mixture. Drop spoonfuls of the reserved batter on top.
8. With a metal skewer, swirl the mixtures to marble. Do not blend completely. Bake for 30-35 minutes, until just set. Unmould when cool and cut into squares for serving.

NOTE: *Most health food shops sell dairy-free soft cheese. These tend to taste more like the real thing than the dairy-free hard cheeses do. (See picture, page fifty-one.)*

Melting Moments

Makes about 10. Takes 30 mins.

2 oz (55g) dairy-free margarine
1½ oz (42g) caster sugar
Few drops of vanilla essence
2½ oz (70g) self-raising flour
2 oz (55g) desiccated coconut
10 pieces of diced papaya

1. Cream the margarine, sugar and essence until light and fluffy.
2. Stir in the flour and mix thoroughly.
3. Divide into 10 pieces, roll each into a ball and roll in the coconut.
4. Place on a greased tray, flatten slightly. Press a piece of diced papaya into the centre of each. Bake at 180°C (350°F) Gas Mark 4, for about 12 minutes.

NOTE: *If you do not have a citrus intolerance, glace cherries can be used instead of papaya. Glace cherries nearly always contain lemon juice.*

Oat Lace Cookies

The problem with these cookies is they soon seem to get eaten!

Makes 36. Takes 30 mins.

5½ oz (155g) dairy-free margarine
6 oz (170g) porridge oats
6 oz (170g) dark brown sugar
6 oz (170g) granulated sugar
3 tbsp (21g) plain flour
Pinch of salt
1 egg, lightly beaten
1 tsp (5ml) vanilla essence

1. Preheat the oven to 180°C (350°F) Gas Mark 4. Grease two baking sheets.
2. Melt the margarine in a small saucepan over a low heat, set aside.
3. In a mixing bowl, combine the oats, brown sugar, granulated sugar, flour and salt.
4. Add the margarine, the egg and vanilla essence and mix until blended.
5. Drop rounded teaspoonfuls of the batter about 2 inch (5cm) apart on the prepared baking sheets. Depending on the size of your baking sheets, probably only half of the mixture will fit. Bake for 5-8 minutes until lightly browned on the edges and bubbling. Leave to cool for 2 minutes, and then transfer to a wire rack to cool completely. Grease the baking sheets and cook the next batch of cookies.

NOTE: *This recipe makes a lot of cookies, but they can be frozen.*

Peppermint Slices

Makes 16. Takes 1 hr including cooling time.

2 oz (55g) dairy-free margarine
2 oz (55g) caster sugar
4 oz (110g) plain flour
6 oz (165g) icing sugar
2 tbsp (28ml) warm water
½ tsp (2½ml) peppermint extract
A few drops of green food colouring (optional)
6 oz (165g) carob

1. Preheat the oven to 180°C (350°F) Gas Mark 4. Line a 12 x 8 inch (30 x 20cm) tin.
2. Beat the margarine and sugar together until light and fluffy. Stir in the flour until the mixture holds together.
3. Knead the mixture to form pliable dough and press into the prepared tin. Prick the surface with a fork. Bake for 10-15 minutes, until lightly browned and just firm to the touch. Remove from the oven and leave to cool in the tin.
4. Sift the icing sugar into a bowl. Stirring, gradually add the water, peppermint extract and food colouring.
5. Spread the icing over the base and leave to cool.
6. Melt the carob in a small bowl set over a saucepan of simmering water. Spread over the icing. Allow to set before cutting up.

Toffee Bars

Makes 16. Takes 30 mins.

6 oz (170g) light brown sugar
8 oz (225g) dairy-free margarine
1 egg yolk
1 tsp (5ml) vanilla essence
8 oz (225g) plain flour
Pinch of salt
4 oz (110g) carob, chopped

1. Preheat the oven to 180°C (350°F) Gas Mark 4. Grease a 13 x 9 x 2 inch (33 x 23 x 5cm) cake tin. Beat together the sugar and margarine until light and fluffy. Beat in the egg yolk and vanilla essence. Stir in the flour and salt.
2. Spread the dough in the prepared cake tin. Bake for 20-25 minutes, until lightly browned. The texture will be soft.
3. Remove from the oven and immediately place the carob pieces on the hot cookie base. Leave to stand until the carob softens, and then spread it evenly with a spatula. While still warm, cut into bars.

NOTE: *Why not make meringues with the leftover egg white?*

Cakes, Puddings & Ice-Cream

Victoria Sandwich Cake

Recipes & Notes

Apple and Blackberry Pie

Serves 6. Takes 1 hr to cook and 15 mins to make the pastry.

8 oz (225g) plain flour / Pinch of salt
2 oz (55g) dairy-free margarine
2 oz (55g) white vegetable fat / 4 tsp (20ml) cold water to mix
1 lb (450g) red apples / 6 oz (170g) blackberries
4 oz (110g) caster sugar / Soya milk to glaze

1. Sift the flour and salt into a bowl. Add the fats cut into small pieces and rub in with your fingertips until the mixture resembles fine breadcrumbs.
2. Add sufficient water to mix to pliable dough, using a round-bladed knife. Add a little water at a time until the dough holds together.
3. Turn out onto a lightly floured flat surface and knead very lightly until evenly mixed. If time allows, wrap in foil and chill for 30 minutes.
4. Roll out just under three-quarters of the pastry and use to line a pie dish.
5. Mix the apples, blackberries and caster sugar together and put in the pastry case.
6. Roll out the remaining pastry for the lid and position on top. Using your thumbs press down the edges of the pie and trim. Make two small slits in the centre. Glaze with the soya milk.
7. Stand the pie on a hot baking sheet and bake at 220°C (425°F) Gas Mark 7 for 15 minutes. Reduce the temperature to 180°C (350°F) Gas Mark 4 and continue cooking for about 30 minutes, or until the pastry is golden brown.
8. Serve hot or cold, sprinkled with sugar.

NOTE: *If you do not have a citrus intolerance, cooking apples can be used instead. If you can find a dairy-free ready-made, short-crust pastry, this can be used. Other fruits can also be used, why not try strawberry or redcurrant?*

Baked Custard

Serves 4. Takes 1 hr 30 mins.

8 oz (225g) plain flour / Pinch of salt
2 oz (55g) dairy-free margarine
2 oz (55g) white vegetable fat
4 tsp (20ml) cold water to mix
3 eggs / 2 tbsp (25g) caster sugar / 1 tsp (5ml) vanilla essence
1 pt (568ml) soya milk / Ground nutmeg to sprinkle

1. Sift the flour and salt into a bowl. Add the fats cut into small pieces and rub in with your fingertips until the mixture resembles fine breadcrumbs.
2. Add sufficient water to mix to pliable dough, using a round-bladed knife. Add a little water at a time until the dough holds together.
3. Turn out onto a lightly floured flat surface and knead very lightly until evenly mixed. If time allows, wrap in foil and chill for 30 minutes.
4. Roll out the pastry and use to line an 8 inch (21cm) diameter round heatproof dish and trim the edges. Cover with greaseproof paper, weighted down with the pastry trimmings. Bake at 180°C (350°F) Gas Mark 4 for about 10 minutes, uncover and bake for another 5 minutes.
5. Put the eggs, sugar and vanilla essence in a bowl and whisk lightly to combine. Heat the soya milk in a pan until just warm and stir into the eggs, mixing well.
6. Strain the mixture through a sieve into the pastry case. Sprinkle with the nutmeg. Put the dish in a baking tin and pour enough hot water in the tin to come halfway up the side of the custard dish.
7. Bake for about 1-1½ hours at 160°C (325°F) Gas Mark 3, or until the custard is set, it shouldn't wobble in the centre when shaken. Remove and serve warm or at room temperature.

Bakewell Tart

Serves 8. Takes 1 hr.

6 oz (170g) plain flour / Pinch of salt
3 tbsp (45ml) cold water to mix
1½ oz (42g) dairy-free margarine / 1½ oz (42g) white vegetable fat
6 tbsp (90ml) strawberry or raspberry jam
4 oz (110g) ground almonds / ¼ tsp (1¼ml) almond essence
4 oz (110g) caster sugar / A little demerara sugar
3 eggs, beaten / 2 oz (55g) dairy free-margarine

1. Sift the flour and salt into a bowl. Add the fats cut into small pieces and rub in with your fingertips until the mixture resembles fine breadcrumbs.
2. Add sufficient water to mix to pliable dough, using a round-bladed knife. Add a little water at a time until the dough holds together.
3. Turn out onto a lightly floured flat surface and knead very lightly until evenly mixed. If time allows, wrap in foil and chill for 30 minutes.
4. Roll out and use to line a 7 inch (18cm) diameter round tin. Decorate the edges using a fork. Spread the jam over the base. Chill while making the filling.
5. To make the filling, beat the ground almonds, sugar, margarine, eggs and almond essence together in a bowl using an electric mixer. Pour the filling over the jam and spread evenly.
6. Bake at 200°C (400°F) Gas Mark 6 for 30 minutes or until the filling is set. Sprinkle Demerara sugar over the top 10 minutes before the end of the cooking time. Serve warm or cold with dairy-free cream or custard.

NOTE: *Jam without citrus products, is very difficult to find, but if you make your own just omit the lemon juice. This makes it slightly runnier.*

Carob Cheesecake

Serves 4. Takes 30 mins plus 2 hrs chilling.

1½ oz (42g) dairy-free margarine
1 oz (28g) demerara sugar
4 oz (110g) digestive biscuits, crushed
5 oz (140g) dairy free soft cheese
1 oz (28g) caster sugar
3 fl oz (85ml) soya cream
2 oz (55g) carob
1 packet of gelatine, or:
2 tbsp (30ml) cold water / 2 tbsp (30ml) agar

1. Melt the margarine in a saucepan, stir in the biscuits and demerara sugar. Press into a 7 inch (18cm) tin. Chill for 15 minutes.
2. Place the soft cheese and sugar in a bowl and beat until smooth, gradually stir in the soya cream. Prepare the gelatine as on the pack or mix the water with the agar and leave until it begins to thicken. Stir into the mixture and pour over the base.
3. Melt the carob in a bowl over a pan of hot water. Pour over the mixture and swirl to give a marbled effect with a skewer.
4. Chill for about 2 hours or until completely set.

OR:

For a fruit cheesecake, omit the carob and puree 6 oz (170g) of fruit with 4 tbsp (60ml) of cold water, push through a fine sieve and pour over the set cheesecake. I tend to use strawberries or raspberries, if using redcurrants you may wish to sweeten to taste by puree-ing a few spoonfuls of icing sugar with the fruit.

NOTE: *Hobnobs are dairy-free and can be used for this recipe. Most health food shops sell dairy-free soft cheese. These tend to taste more like the real thing than the dairy-free hard cheeses do.*

I tend to use agar as an alternative to gelatine as I have beef intolerance. It is made from seaweed and so is a natural alternative to animal based gelatine and can be bought from health food shops. (See picture, page ninety-six.)

Carob Layer Cake

This cake is easy to make but takes time to put together. It is good for a special occasion, why not serve with a fruit coulis. Serves 6. Takes 45 mins.

2 eggs
2½ oz (70g) caster sugar
2½ oz (70g) plain flour
1 oz (28g) carob, grated
For the carob butter cream:
4 oz (110g) dairy-free margarine
5½ oz (155g) icing sugar
1 tbsp (15ml) water / 2 oz (55g) carob

1. Preheat the oven to 180°C (350°F) Gas Mark 4. Grease and flour enough baking sheets to fit six 6 inch (15 cm) circles.
2. Beat the eggs and sugar using an electric mixer, until very thick and mousse-like and a trail is left when the beaters are lifted. (About 7 minutes.)
3. Using a metal spoon, carefully fold in the flour.
4. Spread the mixture onto the circles on the prepared baking sheets and bake for about 7 minutes or until golden brown. You may have to bake them in batches.
5. Using a sharp knife, trim each round while still warm, then transfer to a wire rack to cool.
6. To make the carob butter cream: beat the margarine and half the icing sugar until creamy. Add the remaining sugar and water, beat until smooth. Melt the carob and stir into the mixture.
7. Sandwich the rounds together with the carob butter cream, reserving some for the top. Grate a little carob over the top to decorate.

Cherry Meringue Pudding

Serves 6. Takes 50 mins.

9 oz (255g) digestive biscuits, crushed
3 oz (85g) dairy-free margarine
2 tbsp (14g) plain flour
2 tbsp (25g) caster sugar
13 oz (370g) tin of cherries, without stones
2 eggs separated
4 oz (110g) caster sugar

1. Melt the margarine in a saucepan and mix with the biscuits. Press the mixture into the bottom of a 10 inch (25cm) diameter ceramic round shallow dish. Chill in the fridge for 15 minutes.
2. Mix the flour and sugar, stir in a little of the cherry juice and work to a paste. Mix in the remainder of the juice and bring to the boil in a saucepan. Stir and remove from the heat. Allow to cool.
3. Beat the egg yolks into the juice mixture. Stir in the cherries and pour the mixture over the biscuit base.
4. Whisk the egg whites until stiff and slowly fold in the sugar. Place over the dish and using the back of a spoon, make peaks with the egg whites.
5. Cook at 200°C (400°F) Gas Mark 6 for about 15 minutes or until lightly browned. Serve hot or cold.

NOTE: Hobnobs are dairy-free and can be used for this recipe. Check the tinned cherries are citrus-free, some contain lemon juice. If you do not have a citrus intolerance, pineapple is a good alternative to cherries.

Doughnuts

Kitchen shops sell doughnut pans for making mini doughnuts.
Makes 12. Takes 15 mins.

3 oz (85g) plain flour
½ tsp (2g) baking powder
¼ tsp (1¼g) salt
2 oz (55g) caster sugar
4 tbsp (60ml) soya milk
1 egg, beaten
1 tsp (5ml) olive oil
½ tsp (2½ml) vanilla essence
Extra caster sugar for dusting

1. Preheat the oven to 200°C (400°F) Gas Mark 6. Take a large bowl and sift the flour, baking powder and salt into it. Add the sugar and give it a stir round to combine.
2. In a separate bowl, whisk the soya milk, beaten egg, olive oil and vanilla essence together and add this to the dry ingredients, mixing thoroughly.
3. Brush the doughnut cups with a little oil. Heat in the oven. Using a teaspoon, carefully fill each of the doughnut cups around three-quarters full with the batter. Place in the oven and bake for about 10 minutes, or until firm, but springy to touch.
4. Cool slightly and sprinkle a little caster sugar onto a plate. Turn the doughnuts out and dip them into the sugar.

Fudge

Makes 50 pieces. Takes 45 mins.

½ pt (280ml) soya milk
1¾ lb (850g) caster sugar
4 oz (110g) dairy-free margarine
2 tsp (10ml) vanilla extract

1. Line a 7 inch (18cm) square tin with baking parchment. Pour the soya milk into a large pan and slowly bring to the boil.
2. Add the sugar and margarine and heat slowly, stirring constantly until the sugar has dissolved and the margarine has melted.
3. Bring to the boil and cover the pan. Boil for 2 minutes.
4. Uncover the pan and continue to boil stirring occasionally until it reaches soft ball stage, 116°C (240°F) on a sugar thermometer.
5. Remove from the heat, stir in the vanilla extract and leave to cool for 5 minutes.
6. Beat until it begins to lose its gloss and is thick, about 5 minutes.
7. Pour into the tin and allow to cool before cutting into squares.

NOTE: *A sugar thermometer is needed for this recipe. When boiling sugar, larger quantities work best so this recipe does make quite a lot of fudge. Why not give some to a friend as a present? Golden caster sugar gives a richer colour.*

Golden Syrup Pudding

Serves 4-6 depending on the size of your pudding bowls. Takes 40 mins.

4 oz (110g) dairy-free margarine
4 oz (110g) caster sugar
A few drops of vanilla essence
2 eggs, beaten
4 oz (110g) self-raising flour
6 tbsp (90ml) golden syrup

1. Preheat the oven to 180°C (350°F) Gas Mark 4. Lightly oil 4-6 individual-serving-sized pudding bowls and place a small circle of non-stick baking paper in the base of each one.
2. Place the margarine and sugar in a bowl and beat until pale and creamy. Stir in the vanilla essence. Gradually add the beaten eggs, a little at a time, adding a tablespoon of flour after each addition of egg and beat well.
3. When the mixture is smooth, add the remaining flour and fold in gently. Add a tablespoon of water and mix to form a soft dropping consistency.
4. Spoon enough mixture into each bowl to come halfway up, leaving enough room for rising. Place on a baking sheet and bake in the oven for about 25 minutes until firm and golden brown.
5. Allow the puddings to stand for 5 minutes. Discard the paper circle and turn out on to serving plates.
6. Warm the golden syrup in a saucepan and pour a little over each pudding. Serve hot or cold with dairy-free ice-cream or custard.

Meringue

A good way to use up leftover egg whites. They keep for a long time and can be eaten with ice-cream or served with fruit.

Makes about 24 small meringues or one large one. Takes 2 hrs 10 mins.

4 egg whites
8 oz (225g) caster sugar

1. Put the egg whites in a large grease free bowl. Whisk using a hand-held mixer, until the mixture is thick and white and stands in stiff peaks. Do not over whisk.
2. Whisk in about two-thirds of the sugar, a level tablespoon at a time until completely incorporated and the meringue is stiff again before adding more sugar.
3. Fold in the rest of the sugar a little at a time, using a metal spoon in a figure of eight folding movement.
4. Spoon the meringue onto a greased baking sheet either in small heaps or one large round.
5. Bake for 2 hours at 110°C (225°F) Gas Mark ¼. Leave to cool and store in an airtight container.

NOTE: *Why not pipe the meringue into nest shapes, when cooked fill with dairy-free custard and top with your favourite soft fruit?*

Mint Carob Ice-Cream

When making ice-cream it is important that all the ingredients are chilled beforehand. You can buy chocolate flavoured dairy-free ice-cream but if you have a caffeine intolerance this is not suitable. Try this delicious mint-carob ice-cream.

Serves 5. Takes 50 mins.

2 egg yolks
9 fl oz (255ml) soya milk
5½ fl oz (155ml) soya cream
3 oz (85g) caster sugar
A few drops of peppermint essence
1 oz (28g) chopped carob

1. Beat the egg yolks and the sugar until the mixture is light and frothy.
2. Add the milk, stirring constantly. Whip the cream until it is thick. Stir into the milk mixture.
3. Add the peppermint essence and carob, making sure the ingredients are thoroughly mixed.
4. Either pour into an ice-cream maker and mix until setting around the edge or pour into a shallow container and freeze. Every 15 minutes remove from the freezer and mash with a fork. Repeat this process until the ice-cream is smooth and does not contain ice crystals.

NOTE: Home made ice-cream is best eaten straight away or within a few days.

Pan Fried Bananas

Serves 4. Takes 10 mins.

4 ripe bananas
2 oz (55g) dairy-free margarine
2 oz (55g) light, brown sugar

1. Remove the banana skins and slice in half. Heat the dairy-free margarine gently in a large frying pan. Add the sugar and stir until bubbling.
2. Add the bananas cook until softened on one side and slightly golden and then turn and repeat on the other side.
3. Serve hot with dairy-free ice-cream or dairy-free custard.

Pancakes

Pancakes can be served with fruit, ice-cream or golden syrup.

Serves 4. Takes 10 mins.

4 oz (110g) plain flour
Pinch of salt
1 egg
½ pt (284ml) soya milk
Sunflower oil for frying

1. Sift the flour and salt into a bowl and make a well in the middle.
2. Break the egg into the well and add about half of the liquid.
3. Gradually work the flour into the liquid using a hand whisk. Beat until it is quite smooth.
4. Add the rest of the liquid, a little at a time, again beating until quite smooth.
5. At this stage, the batter may be left to stand for several hours in a cool place before use.
6. Heat a little oil in a thin bottomed frying pan. Once hot, pour in enough batter to thinly cover the bottom of the pan when swirled around. Shake the pan to loosen the pancake as it cooks. Once cooked on one side either flip or use a spatula to turn it and cook on the other side.
7. Serve with your chosen fillings.

Popcorn

If you have a popcorn maker just put the popcorn in without the oil, (this is safer).

Serves 4. Takes 10 minutes.

4 oz (110g) popping corn
4 tbsp (60ml) sunflower oil
Caster sugar, to taste
Golden syrup, to taste

1. Either cook the popcorn in your popcorn maker until it pops, or heat the oil gently in a saucepan until the test corn pops.
2. Remove from the heat, add the corn. Cover and return to the heat until all the corn has popped.
3. Put the corn in a bowl, pour over some golden syrup and mix in. Sprinkle over the sugar to taste and eat whilst still warm

Raspberry Meringue Ice Cream

Serves 4-5. Takes 45 mins.

7 oz (200g) fresh raspberries
2½ oz (65g) caster sugar
1 egg yolk
6 fl oz (170ml) soya milk
2 fl oz (55ml) soya cream
About 4 crumbled meringues

1. Wash the raspberries. Puree them with the milk. Beat the egg yolk with the sugar. Whip the cream until thick.
2. Combine the raspberry mixture, the whipped cream and egg yolks. Make sure that all the ingredients are thoroughly mixed.
3. Either pour into an ice-cream maker and mix until setting around the edge. Or pour into a shallow container and freeze. Every 15 minutes remove from the freezer and mash with a fork. Repeat this process until the ice-cream is smooth and does not contain ice crystals.
4. Just before the ice-cream is completely set stir in the meringue.

NOTE: *The strawberries can be substituted with raspberries, blackberries or a combination of summer fruits. Home made ice-cream is best eaten within a few days.*

Rhubarb and Apple Crumble

Serves 4. Takes 40 mins.

10 oz (300g) rhubarb, chopped
3 red apples, peeled, cored and chopped
5 oz (150g) granulated sugar
½ tsp (2½g) ground ginger
2 oz (55g) plain flour
1 oz (28g) wholemeal plain flour
3 oz (85g) muscovado sugar
2 oz (55g) ground almonds
2 oz (55g) dairy-free margarine

1. Preheat the oven to 200°C (400°F) Gas Mark 6 and warm a baking tray.
2. Place the rhubarb and apples in a pie dish. Sprinkle the sugar and ginger over the top.
3. Mix together the flours, muscovado sugar and almonds in a bowl. Rub in the margarine and press on top of the fruit mixture.
4. Bake in the oven, placing the pie dish on the preheated baking tray for about 30 minutes, or until golden brown.

NOTE: *Serve warm with custard made using soya milk. If you do not have a citrus intolerance, use cooking apples instead.*

Strawberry Ice-Cream

It is possible to buy very good dairy-free fruit ice-cream, but it always contains lemon juice so is not suitable for people who have a citrus intolerance.

Serves 5. Takes 45 mins.

7 oz (200g) fresh strawberries
2¼ oz (65g) caster sugar
1 egg yolk
6 fl oz (170ml) soya milk
2 fl oz (55ml) soya cream

1. Wash the strawberries. Puree them together with the milk. Beat the egg yolk with the sugar. Whip the cream until thick.
2. Combine the strawberry mixture, the whipped cream and egg yolk mixture. Make sure that all the ingredients are thoroughly mixed.
3. Either pour into an ice-cream maker and mix until setting around the edge or pour into a shallow container and freeze. Every 15 minutes remove from the freezer and mash with a fork. Repeat this process until the ice-cream is smooth and does not contain ice crystals.

NOTE: *The strawberries can be substituted with raspberries, blackberries or a combination of summer fruits. Homemade ice-cream is best eaten within a few days.*

Strawberry Mousse Ice-Cream

This recipe takes a little longer to make but gives a softer mousse-like texture to the ice cream. Serves 5. Takes 1hr 30 mins.

7 fl oz (175ml) water
7 oz (200g) caster sugar
7 oz (200g) strawberries
2 egg whites
1 fl oz (25ml) soya cream

1. Put the water and sugar into a pan and whilst heating stir constantly to dissolve the sugar.
2. Boil the sugar syrup for 1 minute. Remove from the heat and allow to cool completely. This will take a while as it needs to be at fridge temperature before use.
3. Puree the strawberries with the cooled sugar syrup.
4. Beat the egg whites until almost stiff.
5. Stir the strawberry mixture into the beaten egg whites and then pour in the cream. Mix thoroughly.
6. Either pour into an ice-cream maker and mix until setting around the edge. Or pour into a shallow container and freeze. Every 15 minutes remove from the freezer and mash with a fork. Repeat this process until the ice-cream is smooth and does not contain ice crystals.

NOTE: *The strawberries can be substituted with other summer fruit. Home made ice-cream is best eaten within a few days.*

Victoria Sandwich Cake

Serves 10. Takes 35 mins.

6 oz (170g) dairy-free margarine
6 oz (170g) caster sugar
3 large eggs
6 oz (170g) self-raising flour
A few drops of vanilla essence
1 tbsp (15ml) cold water
For the filling:
2 oz (55g) dairy-free margarine
4 oz (110g) icing sugar
1 tbsp (15ml) soya milk
3 tbsp (33g) jam

1. Grease two 8 inch (20cm) diameter round sandwich or layer cake tins and line the bases with greased, wax or greaseproof paper.
2. Put the margarine and sugar in a bowl and cream together using a wooden spoon until the mixture is very light and fluffy and pale in colour.
3. Beat in the eggs, one at a time, until completely incorporated and follow each with a tablespoon (6g) of the flour.
4. Sift the remaining flour and fold into the creamed mixture, using a metal spoon for preference, alternating with the essence and the water. The mixture should be a soft dropping consistency.
5. Divide between the tins and level the tops, spreading out from the centre with a round-bladed knife, but only very lightly. Do not push out all the air that has been incorporated.
6. Bake at 190°C (375°F) Gas Mark 5, for about 20-25 minutes or until well risen and firm to the touch.
7. Cool in the tin briefly until the sides of the cakes begin to shrink from the tin and then turn out onto a wire rack and leave until cool.
8. Cream the margarine until very soft, beat in the icing sugar, adding the soya milk to make a spreading consistency. Spread over one of the cakes and sandwich together along with the jam. Dust the top with icing sugar.

NOTE: *Jam without citrus products is very difficult to find, but if you make your own just omit the lemon juice. This makes it slightly runnier. If you cannot get any jam why not just sandwich the cakes with the butter cream and then cover the top of the cake with carob. This recipe can also be used to make about 24 buns.*

To make a chocolate version replace 1 oz (28g) of the flour with carob powder (or cocoa if you do not have a caffeine intolerance) and add ½ tsp (2g) of baking powder. Sieve both with the flour. (See picture page seventy-five and chocolate/carob version, page six.)

First published in Great Britain by:

Ashgrove Publishing

an imprint of:
Hollydata Publishers Ltd
27 John Street
London WC1N 2BX

ISBN 978 185398 163 0

First Edition

Book design by Brad Thompson
Printed and bound in China